Contents

D1494473

▶ Short walks

Introduction

Durdle Door

Walking in Dorset

Dorset offers an amazing variety of unspoilt scenery and many wonderful opportunities for walking. There are no mountains but there are high places with magnificent views. The county is rich in geology and wildlife.

The gentle, undulating countryside around Blackmoor Vale and the River Stour contrasts vividly with the heathland of mid-Dorset and the outstanding natural beauty of the rugged coastline. Rolling chalk hills with ridge-top footpaths provide splendid walking; so does the Dorset Coast Path with its huge cliffs and interesting features such as Golden Cap, Durdle Door and Chesil Beach. The coast is the most popular area for visitors so venture inland if you seek remote and quiet places.

The county has a fascinating history too, dominated by the remains of prehistory. Hillforts, tumuli, earthworks and other ancient monuments are scattered across the countryside. There are also many delightful villages and country towns which are well worth visiting.

Dorset is linked inextricably with Thomas Hardy, the poet and novelist, who was born in Higher Bockhampton in 1840 and lived most of his life in the county. Hardy adopted the name of the Saxon kingdom of Wessex to give territorial definition to the world his characters inhabited and to unite his series of novels. Hardy's Wessex was an evocation of the Dorset landscape he knew so well, 'partly real, partly dream-country'. Lovers of Hardy's novels and poems come here from all over the world, and an awareness of his work will add immensely to the appreciation of this area, whilst enabling the walker, travelling in a way thoroughly recommended by Hardy, to really get to know 'remarkably well' this 'little bit of the world'.

Walking is a pastime which can fulfil the needs of everyone. You can adapt it to suit your own preferences and it is one of the healthiest of activities. This guide is for those who just want to walk a few miles. It really doesn't take long to find yourself in some lovely countryside. All the walks are five miles or less so should easily be completed in under three hours. Walking can be anything from an individual pastime to a family stroll, or maybe a group of friends enjoying the fresh air and open spaces of our countryside. There is no need for walking to be competitive and, to get the most from a walk, it shouldn't be regarded simply as a means of covering a given distance in the shortest possible time.

What is Dorset?

Dorset is a predominately rural county in southwest England bounded by Devon, Somerset, Wiltshire, Hampshire, Bournemouth, Poole and the English Channel. It has many small villages but few large urban or industrial areas and no motorways. The county town is Dorchester which is adjoined by the new urban development of Poundbury designed by the Prince of Wales. Traditional market towns of note include Shaftesbury, Sturminster Newton, Blandford Forum and Wimborne Minster, whilst on the coast are the holiday resorts of Lyme Regis, Bridport, Weymouth and Swanage. The Stour, Frome and Piddle or Trent are among numerous small rivers which which cut green fertile valleys.

One unique area of Dorset is the Isle of Purbeck; although described as an island it is in reality a peninsular of around 60 square miles (155sq.km) with water on three sides, the English Channel, the River Frome and Poole Harbour.

Dorset is noted for its agricultural and dairy produce and for Portland Stone, a white-grey limestone which has been used extensively as a building stone, notably in major public buildings in London such as Buckingham Palace and St Paul's Cathedral. Stone has been quarried in the Isle of Portland and the Isle of Purbeck since the Middle Ages. Tourism is very important to the economy of Dorset and has developed due to the beautiful scenery and coastline, the proliferation of prehistoric remains and the connection with Thomas Hardy.

Dorset countryside from Whiteways Hill

The county has a long history of human settlement. Cave dwellers lived in the area in the middle of the Ice Age, about half a million years ago, while agriculture has been dated back to 4000 BC. By about 500 BC present day Dorset was the territory of the Durotriges, who built impressive hillforts, such as that at Maiden Castle just outside Dorchester. They could not stop the Romans, however, who established their culture here for 400 years and founded the town of Dunrovia (Dorchester).

Geology

The varied Dorset landscape is due to its fascinating underlying geology. There are a number of large ridges of limestone which include a band of chalk which crosses the county from southwest to northeast including Cranborne Chase, the Dorset Downs and the Purbeck Hills. Between the limestone downland ridges are large, wide clay valleys with broad flood plains including the Blackmoor Vale (Stour Valley) and Frome Valley.

Southeast Dorset lies on non-resistant Eocene clays, sands and gravels, the thin soils supporting a heathland habitat. The River Frome estuary runs through this weak rock and its many tributaries have carved out a wide estuary. At the mouth of the estuary sand spits have been deposited turning the estuary into Poole Harbour. The harbour and the chalk and limestone hills of the Purbecks to the south lie above Europe's largest onshore oil field.

Most of the Dorset coast (together with part of the East Devon coast) was listed as an UNESCO World Heritage Site in 2001 because of its impressive geological formations and textbook examples of features of coastal erosion. The coast represents much of the Mesozoic era (251-66 million years ago) with a sequence of Triassic, Jurassic and Cretaceous rock exposures and it is commonly known as 'The Jurassic Coast'. It has yielded a large number of animal and plant fossils including flying reptiles, marine reptiles and dinosaur footprints. The notable landforms include the sea stacks near Handfast Point, the cove at Lulworth and the natural arch of Durdle Door. The limestone island of Portland is connected to the mainland by the 18 mile pebble tombolo of Chesil Beach. The Fleet Lagoon, which Chesil Beach encloses, is one of the most important saline lagoons in Europe.

In the west of Dorset the chalk and clay begins to give way to marl and granite, more characteristic of the geology of Devon.

Wildlife in Dorset

The variety found in the Dorset landscape is reflected in its wildlife. Added to which, the southerly location and relatively warm climate make it possible for many species to survive compared with places further north in Britain. All six native species of reptile can be found here. The fragments of heathland left in Dorset are home to many rare plants and animals. In summer you may see an emperor dragonfly, or a silver-studded blue butterfly. The smooth snake, one of Britain's rarest reptiles, has its home on the open heathland together with the sand lizard, while a marsh gentian may be seen amidst thicker vegetation. On the limestone cliffs, in summer, look out for the adonis blue butterfly. Gulls, including kittiwakes, abound along the coast and the coastline provides many breeding grounds for seabirds, as well as habitats for overwintering birds. Portland Bill is a major bird migration point, spring or autumn being the best time to witness this spectacle. In summer the flocks of mute swans can be seen at Abbotsbury. Poole Harbour is a feeding ground for many birds, including a large colony of black-headed gulls. Information on wildlife in Dorset can be obtained from the Dorset Wildlife Trust as well as the location of nature reserves within the county.

Hardy's Wessex

Thomas Hardy was convinced that 'it is better for a writer to know a little bit of the world remarkably well than to know a great part of the world remarkably little'. His little bit of the world was Dorset and the surrounding counties, which became his fictionalised Wessex. County boundaries were disregarded, while towns and villages were renamed, often transparently, giving Hardy his own stage upon which his stories were set. Hardy's Wessex became vividly detailed, making its exploration fascinating.

The landscape of Hardy's Wessex is far from uniform. Its variety is striking, from the Vale of the Little Dairies to the wilds of Egdon Heath and the inspiring Wessex Heights. Its core is Hardy's native parish of Stinsford (the 'Mellstock' of the novels). Hardy was born here in a cottage at Higher Bockhampton in 1840. This was then a wild, lonely place where 'snakes and efts swarmed in the summer days, and nightly bats would fly about our bedrooms'. The most prominent features of Hardy's boyhood environment were the Heath and the River Frome, which separates Bockhampton from the county town of Dorchester. Hardy gave the individual heaths, which extend to Poole Harbour, the collective name of Egdon Heath, where the outlook was 'lone and bare'. The wild beauty of this excited Hardy's imagination, especially in *The Return of the Native*, where Clym Yeobright 'was permeated with its scenes, with its substance, and with its odours'. In *The Mayor of Casterbridge*, Hardy described the heath as 'that ancient country whose surface never had been stirred to a finger's depth, save by the scratching of rabbits, since brushed by the feet of the earliest tribes'. Only small pockets of this heathland have survived the agricultural improvements and the dense conifer afforestation of the 20th century,

The River Frome flows eastwards to Poole Harbour. Its green, fertile valley was where the waters 'were as clear as the pure River of Life shown to the Evangelist, rapid as the shadow of a cloud, with pebbly shallows that prattled to the sky all day long'. In autumn the river filled up and 'the smallest gullies were all full; there was no taking short cuts anywhere, and foot passengers were compelled to follow the permanent ways'. Angel Clare courted Tess here, 'in the valley her spirits up wonderfully' upon first sight. This is still a lush, dairy-farming landscape, although the milkmaids have been replaced by machines. Here was a rich seam from which Hardy could link the environment with human emotions, as in *Tess of the d'Urbervilles*: 'Amid the oozing fatness and warm ferments of the Froom Vale, at a season when the rush of juices could almost be heard below the hiss of fertilization, it was impossible that the most fanciful love should not grow passionate. The ready bosoms existing there were impregnated by their surroundings'.

The Vale of Blackmoor, or Blackmore, was the home of Tess. Its gateway is Sturminster Newton, past which flows the River Stour and it is best seen from the surrounding heights. The river and its tributaries give the vale its character, enhanced by the villages which cluster on islands of higher ground above land liable to flooding. Hardy wrote in *The Woodlanders* that the Vale 'cannot be regarded as inferior to any inland scenery of the sort in the west of England, or perhaps anywhere in the Kingdom'. The heavy clay soil is the kind where Hardy felt 'superstitions linger longest'. The trees relate to humans, as in *The Woodlanders*, when Marty South remarked that the young pines she was planting seemed to 'sigh because they are very sorry to begin life in earnest - just as we be'.

The downland ridges of Dorset were Hardy's Wessex Heights, 'where men have never cared to haunt nor women have walked with me, and ghosts then keep their distance; and I know some liberty'. The north Dorset escarpment overlooking the Vale of Blackmore constantly recurs in the novels. Here is the scene of Tess's poverty-stricken winter at Flintcombe-Ash, 'a starve-acre place' where 'Tess slaved in the morning frosts and in the afternoon rains'. Not far from here is the Giant of Cerne Abbas, the 'Cernel Giant' who ate babies in ancient times, according to Mrs Cantle in *The Dynasts*. This is also sheep country and Hardy wrote of the sheepfair at 'Greenhilll' (Woodbury Hill) outside 'Kingsbere' (Bere Regis), the annual gathering on the top of a hill attended by 'multitude after multitude' of 'horned and hornless' sheep. Nearby is Tolpuddle, the home of the trade union Martyrs. Their trial was held in Dorchester, Hardy's 'Casterbridge' and the town most closely associated with the novelist.

Dorset poppy field

Hardy's Wessex also has fine coastal scenery. Weymouth was only 10 miles (16km) from Hardy's home and he was fond of 'the boats, the sands, the esplanade'. Hardy wrote *Desperate Remedies*, his first published novel, in Weymouth, but *The Trumpet Major* and *The Dynasts* are the fruits of a longer association with the coast. Hardy's grandparents remembered when this coastline was under threat of invasion by Napoleon, and folk-memories and legends from the time enliven Hardy's works. *The Hand of Ethelberta* is the novel of Purbeck. This 'isle' is a microcosm of the Dorset landscape, with chalk, clay, limestone, sand and shale, rugged and gentle scenery. It is reached through the gap guarded by Corfe Castle which, like the cliffs and headlands of Purbeck, was visited frequently by Hardy. The newly-married Thomas and Emma Hardy walked the cliffs east of Swanage, where the detached stumps of chalk stand witness to the power of the waves. Further west, towards Weymouth, the spectacular cove at Lulworth is where Sergeant Troy was thought to have drowned in *Far from the Madding Crowd*.

Walking tips & guidance

Safety

As with all other outdoor activities, walking is safe provided a few simple commonsense rules are followed:

* Make sure you are fit enough to complete the walk;

* Always try to let others know where you intend going, especially if you are walking alone;

* Be clothed adequately for the weather and always wear suitable footwear;

* Always allow plenty of time for the walk, especially if it is longer or harder than you have done before;

* Whatever the distance you plan to walk, always allow plenty of daylight hours unless you are absolutely certain of the route;

* If mist or bad weather come on unexpectedly, do not panic but instead try to remember the last certain feature which you have passed (road, farm, wood, etc.). Then work out your route from that point on the map but be sure of your route before continuing;

* Do not dislodge stones on the high edges: there may be climbers or other walkers on the lower crags and slopes;

* Unfortunately, accidents can happen even on the easiest of walks. If this should be the case and you need the help of others, make sure that the injured person is safe in a place where no further injury

is likely to occur. For example, the injured person should not be left on a steep hillside or in danger from falling rocks. If you have a mobile phone and there is a signal, call for assistance. If, however, you are unable to contact help by mobile and you cannot leave anyone with the injured person, and even if they are conscious, try to leave a written note explaining their injuries and whatever you have done in the way of first aid treatment. Make sure you know exactly where you left them and then go to find assistance. Make your way to a telephone, dial 999 and ask for the police or mountain rescue. Unless the accident has happened within easy access of a road, it is the responsibility of the police to arrange evacuation. Always give accurate directions on how to find the casualty and, if possible, give an indication of the injuries involved;

- When walking in open country, learn to keep an eye on the immediate foreground while you admire the scenery or plan the route ahead. This may sound difficult but will enhance your walking experience;

- It's best to walk at a steady pace, always on the flat of the feet as this is less tiring. Try not to walk directly up or downhill. A zigzag route is a more comfortable way of negotiating a slope. Running directly downhill is a major cause of erosion on popular hillsides;

- When walking along a country road, walk on the right, facing the traffic. The exception to this rule is, when approaching a blind bend, the walker should cross over to the left and so have a clear view and also be seen in both directions;

- Finally, always park your car where it will not cause inconvenience to other road users or prevent a farmer from gaining access to his fields. Take any valuables with you or lock them out of sight in the car.

Equipment

Equipment, including clothing, footwear and rucksacks, is essentially a personal thing and depends on several factors, such as the type of activity planned, the time of year, and weather likely to be encountered.

All too often, a novice walker will spend money on a fashionable jacket but will skimp when it comes to buying footwear or a comfortable rucksack. Blistered and tired feet quickly remove all enjoyment from even the most exciting walk and a poorly balanced rucksack will soon feel as though you are carrying a ton of bricks. Well designed equipment is not only more comfortable but, being better made, it is longer lasting.

Clothing should be adequate for the day. In summer, remember to protect your head and neck, which are particularly vulnerable in a strong sun and use sun screen. Wear light woollen socks and lightweight boots or strong shoes. A spare pullover and waterproofs carried in the rucksack should, however, always be there in case you need them.

Winter wear is a much more serious affair. Remember that once the body starts to lose heat, it becomes much less efficient. Jeans are particularly unsuitable for winter wear and can sometimes even be downright dangerous.

Waterproof clothing is an area where it pays to buy the best you can afford. Make sure that the jacket is loose-fitting, windproof and has a generous hood. Waterproof overtrousers will not only offer complete protection in the rain but they are also windproof. Do not be misled by flimsy nylon 'showerproof' items. Remember, too, that garments made from rubberised or plastic material are heavy to carry and wear and they trap body condensation. Your rucksack should have wide, padded carrying straps for comfort.

It is important to wear boots that fit well or shoes with a good moulded sole – blisters can ruin any walk! Woollen socks are much more comfortable than any other fibre. Your clothes should be comfortable and not likely to catch on twigs and bushes.

It is important to carry a compass, preferably one of the 'Silva' type as well as this guide. A smaller scale map covering a wider area can add to the enjoyment of a walk. Binoculars are not essential but are very useful for spotting distant stiles and give added interest to viewpoints and wildlife. Although none of the walks in this guide venture too far from civilisation, on a hot day even the shortest of walks can lead to dehydration so a bottle of water is advisable.

Finally, a small first aid kit is an invaluable help in coping with cuts and other small injuries.

Public Rights of Way

In 1949, the National Parks and Access to the Countryside Act tidied up the law covering rights of way. Following public consultation, maps were drawn up by the Countryside Authorities of England and Wales to show all the rights of way. Copies of these maps are available for public inspection and are invaluable when trying to resolve doubts over little-used footpaths. Once on the map, the right of way is irrefutable.

Right of way means that anyone may walk freely on a defined footpath or ride a horse or pedal cycle along a public bridleway. No one may interfere with this right and the walker is within his rights if he removes any obstruction along the route, provided that he has not set out purposely with the intention of removing that obstruction. All obstructions should be reported to the local Highways Authority.

In England and Wales rights of way fall into three main categories:

- Public Footpaths – for walkers only;

- Bridleways – for passage on foot, horseback, or bicycle;

- Byways – for all the above and for motorized vehicles

Free access to footpaths and bridleways does mean that certain guidelines should be followed as a courtesy to those who live and work in the area. For example, you should only sit down to picnic where it does not interfere with other walkers or the landowner. All gates must be kept closed to prevent stock from straying and dogs must be kept under close control – usually this is interpreted as meaning that they should be kept on a leash. Motor vehicles must not be driven along a public footpath or bridleway without the landowner's consent.

A farmer can put a docile mature beef bull with a herd of cows or heifers, in a field crossed by a public footpath. Beef bulls such as Herefords (usually brown/red colour) are unlikely to be upset by passers by but dairy bulls, like the black and white Friesian, can be dangerous by nature. It is, therefore, illegal for a farmer to let a dairy bull roam loose in a field open to public access.

The Countryside and Rights of Way Act 2000 (the 'right to roam') allows access on foot to areas of legally defined 'open country' – mountain, moor, downland, heath and registered common land. You will find these areas shaded orange on the maps in this guide. It does not allow freedom to walk anywhere. It also increases protection for Sites of Special Scientific Interest, improves wildlife enforcement legislation and allows better management of Areas of Outstanding Natural Beauty.

Dorset countryside

The Country Code

The Country Code has been designed not as a set of hard and fast rules, although they do have the backing of the law, but as a statement of commonsense. The code is a gentle reminder of how to behave in the countryside. Walkers should walk with the intention of leaving the place exactly as it was before they arrived. There is a saying that a good walker 'leaves only footprints and takes only photographs', which really sums up the code perfectly.

Never walk more than two abreast on a footpath as you will erode more ground by causing an unnatural widening of paths. Also try to avoid the spread of trodden ground around a boggy area. Mud soon cleans off boots but plant life is slow to grow back once it has been worn away.

Have respect for everything in the countryside, be it those beautiful flowers found along the way or a farmer's gate which is difficult to close.

Stone walls were built at a time when labour costs were a fraction of those today and the special skills required to build or repair them have almost disappeared. Never climb over or onto stone walls; always use stiles and gates.

Dogs which chase sheep can cause them to lose their lambs and a farmer is within his rights if he shoots a dog which he believes is worrying his stock.

The moors and woodlands are often tinder dry in summer, so take care not to start a fire. A fire caused by something as simple as a discarded cigarette can burn for weeks, once it gets deep down into the underlying peat.

When walking across fields or enclosed land, make sure that you read the map carefully and avoid trespassing. As a rule, the line of a footpath or right of way, even when it is not clearly defined on the ground, can usually be followed by lining up stiles or gates.

Obviously flowers and plants encountered on a walk should not be taken but left for others passing to enjoy. To use the excuse 'I have only taken a few' is futile. If everyone only took a few the countryside would be devastated. If young wild animals are encountered they should be left well alone. For instance, if a fawn or a deer calf is discovered lying still in the grass it would be wrong to assume that it has been abandoned. Mothers hide their offspring while they go away to graze and browse and return to them at feeding time. If the animals are touched it could mean that they will be abandoned as the human scent might deter the mother from returning to her offspring. Similarly with baby birds, who have not yet mastered flight; they may appear to have been abandoned but often are being watched by their parents who might be waiting for a walker to pass on before coming out to give flight lesson two!

What appear to be harmful snakes should not be killed because firstly the 'snake' could be a slow worm, which looks like a snake but is really a harmless legless lizard, and second, even if it were an adder (they are quite common) it will escape if given the opportunity. Adders are part of the pattern of nature and should not be persecuted. They rarely bite unless they are handled; a foolish act, which is not uncommon; or trodden on, which is rare, as the snakes are usually basking in full view and are very quick to escape.

Map reading

Some people find map reading so easy that they can open a map and immediately relate it to the area of countryside in which they are standing. To others, a map is as unintelligible as ancient Greek! A map is an accurate but flat picture of the three-dimensional features of the countryside. Features such as roads, streams, woodland and buildings are relatively easy to identify, either from their shape or position. Heights, on the other hand, can be difficult to interpret from the single dimension of a map. The Ordnance Survey 1:25,000 mapping used in this guide shows the contours at 5 metre intervals. Summits and spot heights are also shown.

The best way to estimate the angle of a slope, as shown on any map, is to remember that if the contour lines come close together then the slope is steep – the closer together the contours the steeper the slope.

Learn the symbols for features shown on the map and, when starting out on a walk, line up the map with one or more features, which are recognisable both from the map and on the ground. In this way, the map will be correctly positioned relative to the terrain. It should then only be necessary to look from the map towards the footpath or objective of your walk and then make for it! This process is also useful for determining your position at any time during the walk.

Let's take the skill of map reading one stage further: sometimes there are no easily recognisable features nearby: there may be the odd clump of trees and a building or two but none of them can be related exactly to the map. This is a frequent occurrence but there is a simple answer to the problem and this is where the use of a compass comes in. Simply place the map on the ground, or other flat surface, with the compass held gently above the map. Turn the map until the edge is parallel to the line of the compass needle, which should point to the top of the map. Lay the compass on the map and adjust the position of both, making sure that the compass needle still points to the top of the map and is parallel to the edge. By this method, the map is orientated in a north-south alignment. To find your position on the map, look out for prominent features and draw imaginary lines from them down on to the map. Your position is where these lines cross. This method of map reading takes a little practice before you can become proficient but it is worth the effort.

How to use this book

This book contains route maps and descriptions for 20 walks, with areas of interest indicated by symbols (see below). For each walk particular points of interest are denoted by a number both in the text and on the map (where the number appears in a circle). In the text the route instructions are prefixed by a capital letter. We recommend that you read the whole description, including the fact box at the start of each walk, before setting out.

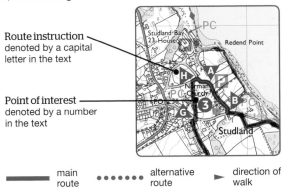

Route instruction
denoted by a capital
letter in the text

Point of interest
denoted by a number
in the text

| ▬▬▬ | main route | •••••••• | alternative route | ▶ | direction of walk |

Key to walk symbols
At the start of each walk there is a series of symbols that indicate particular areas of interest associated with the route.

🐦 Birdlife	🐾 Other wildlife	❀ Wild flowers
🔅 Good views	🏛 Historical interest	🌳 Woodland
⛏ Geology	📖 Literature	

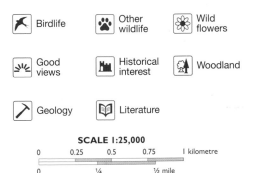

SCALE 1:25,000

0   0.25   0.5   0.75   1 kilometre

0   ¼   ½ mile

Please note the scale for walk maps is 1:25,000 unless otherwise stated
North is always at the top of the page

66 Melbury Beacon provides some of the finest views in Dorset **99**

Melbury Beacon is 863ft (263m) high and affords magnificent views north to Shaftesbury and east over Cranborne Chase. There is an Iron Age earthwork around its summit.

View of Cranborne Chase

Melbury Beacon

Wildflowers, Cranborne Chase

Route instructions

A Start from the car park near the summit of Spread Eagle Hill south of Shaftesbury. Take a stile on to National Trust land at Fontmell Down. Go ahead, with a fence on your left.

1 Fontmell Down is rich in butterflies and chalkland flora.

B Cross an old dyke and continue past a stile in the fence on your left. When you reach the end of the trees on your left, veer right downhill, passing an old parish boundary stone.

C Go through a gate near the foot of the hill and walk along the left-hand edge of the field to the fence ahead. Turn right to walk with

the fence on your left. Go though a gate and continue.

D Go through a small gate to follow a path which bears left to a lane in the village of Compton Abbas. Turn right along this lane.

E Fork right and then follow the lane around a sharp left bend to turn right at a T-junction towards East Compton.

2 The 15th century church of St Mary's in East Compton was demolished in 1867. Notice the gargoyles on the remains of the tower and the steps of the old cross in the churchyard.

F Continue along the lane, which bends to the left and

Plan your walk

DISTANCE: 5 miles (8km)

TIME: 2½ hours

START/END: ST886187 Car parking area near the top of Spread Eagle Hill

TERRAIN: Moderate; one steep climb

MAPS: OS Explorer 118; OS Landranger 183

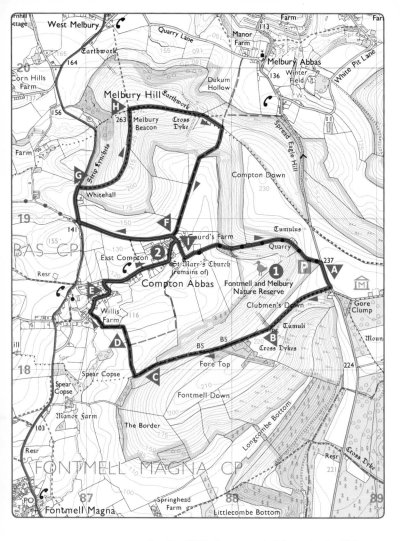

reaches the A350 after 600yds (549m). Take great care as you turn right along the main road past Apple Lynchet and Whitehall.

G Turn right along a track, then pass through a gate to follow a track which gradually climbs beside a hedge and fence on your right to a gate. Go through and follow the track as it bends left uphill. When the track becomes indistinct continue straight up and

Melbury Beacon

through a second gate, to the summit of Melbury Hill. This is the site of the old Beacon.

▶ Continue across a stile and turn right, with Shaftesbury to your left. Follow the fence on your right and down to a bridleway signpost. Turn right through a gate in the fence and walk ahead to join a track. Continue downhill passing through two waymarked gates. Continue with the hedge on your right to join a track which leads to a lane. Turn left.

▶ As the lane bends sharp right, go ahead up a lane marked 'unsuitable for motors'. This lane leads back to the car park.

National Trust sign

66 This is a walk through superb countryside with wonderful views over the New Forest. The walk follows the edge of Bokerley Dyke, a defensive earthwork that now forms part of the border between Dorset and Hampshire 99

Pentridge was renamed 'Trantridge' by Thomas Hardy in his novel *Tess of the d'Urbervilles*. Tess was a farm worker here, while Alec d'Urberville lived in Trantridge with his widowed mother. Tess walked the tracks from here to 'Chaseborough' (Cranborne) for some Saturday night fun at the fair.

Bokerley Dyke

Long Barrow at Bokerley Down

Route instructions

A Park your car in Pentridge and start the walk from the church. With the church behind you, cross the village green to go through a small gate ahead. Continue with the hedge on your left to a gate which gives access to the road.

1 Where the path reaches the road it crosses the course of the Dorset Cursus, of which little remains. This is a Neolithic (New Stone Age) earthwork running northeast from near Blandford Forum and is one of the largest prehistoric monuments in Britain. It consists of two parallel banks about 90yds (82m) apart and seems to have been a forerunner of

the stone avenues such as those at Avebury.

B Turn left along the road until it turns left. Turn right at this corner to follow a green lane. Keep right when you reach a fork.

C Continue ahead, ignoring the cross-track. Follow the downland path to the great earthwork of Bokerley Dyke. A short distance beyond the Martin Down National Nature Reserve notice, turn right to walk on the Hampshire side of the Dyke.

2 Bokerley Dyke, or Ditch, is an impressive earthwork dating back to AD 367 when Britons clashed with Saxons towards the end of

walk 2

Plan your walk

DISTANCE: 4 miles (6.5km)

TIME: 2 hours

START/END: SU034177 Pentridge

TERRAIN: Easy / Moderate

MAPS: OS Explorer 118; OS Landranger 184

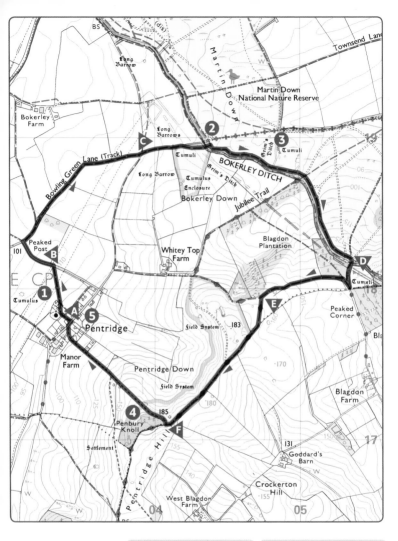

the Roman occupation. The ditch ran for 4 miles (6.4km) cutting across the Roman road between Badbury Rings and Old Sarum. It successfully kept the Saxons out of Dorset for about 150 years.

3 The less impressive earthwork leading off at a right angle from Bokerley Dyke is known as Grim's Ditch. It is older than Bokerley Dyke and may have been constructed in the Bronze Age.

Bokerley Dyke

Turn right along the chalk track, cutting through the Dyke. After 100yds (90m) turn sharp right along the track waymarked with blue arrows. Turn left off this after 50yds (45m) through a small gate waymarked with blue arrows. Walk with a fence on your right through trees to emerge overlooking the Dyke going away on your right. Keep the fence on your right until you reach the corner of a field.

Continue to the trees on the right and to a signpost. Bear left across the field to a group of ash trees. Go through the gate behind the trees to walk with the hedge and views over the New Forest on your left.

Turn right through the trees when you reach Penbury Knoll and descend to cross a stile in a fence.

Continue ahead across the field to cross another stile. Follow the hedged track and then bear right to a stile giving access to the road. Turn right to return to your car.

4 Penbury Knowle is crowned by a simple single ditch Iron Age hillfort.

5 Pentridge is a sleepy little village. The influence of Bokerley Dyke may have led to Pentridge church being dedicated to the Celtic St Rumbold. There is a memorial on the north wall of the nave to the great-great-grandfather of the poet Robert Browning, also known as Robert Browning, who died in 1746.

Long Barrow at Martin Down

Apart from the ancient monument, this is an oasis of natural downland, having been restored to sheep grazing after scrub clearance carried out by the Prince's Trust in 1984. It is also a popular picnic venue, but you can escape the crowds by following the clear tracks from Badbury Rings.

Footpath east of
Badbury Rings

Badbury Rings

East side of Badbury Rings

Route instructions

A Start at the car park west of Badbury Rings, signposted on your right as you come along the B3082 4 miles (6.4km) northwest of Wimborne. Walk along the track which leads from the top corner of the car park furthest away from the Rings. Ignore gates in the fence on your right.

B Go down through a belt of trees and around a gate to walk along a hedged track to an oak wood.

C At the cross-track turn left and immediately right to follow the waymarked path around the edge of the oak woodland to a track.

1 The Oaks, originally known as Sterley Bushes,

is an oak wood over 700 years old and a rare woodland habitat. It was used to provide shelter and grazing for young cattle and is now managed by the National Trust.

D Turn right at the signpost along the track with the wood on your right. This is the course of Ackling Dyke, the Roman road.

E Continue along the track past a farm on your left.

2 This is Ackling Dyke, the Roman road from Dorchester to Old Sarum. It was intersected by a road from Poole Harbour to Bath just to the north-east of the Rings. This is probably the location of

Plan your walk

DISTANCE: 3 miles (4.5km)

TIME: 1½ hours

START/END: ST959032 Car park at Badbury Rings

TERRAIN: Easy

MAPS:
OS Explorer 118;
OS Landranger 195

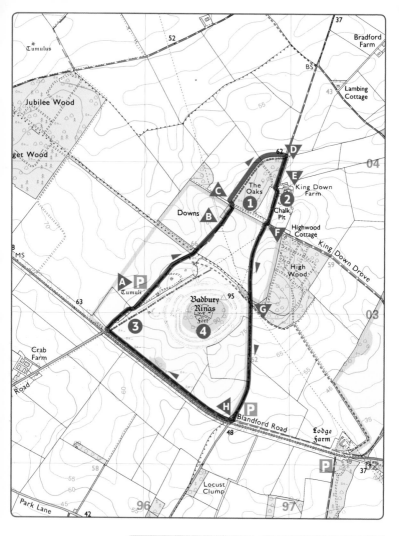

the Roman settlement of Vindocladia (White Ditches). The 'agger' or metalled surface of the Roman road stands 6ft (1.8m) high and is between 40ft (12m) and 50ft (15m) wide. Ackling Dyke was probably raised as early as AD 90 and was a great highway for 300 years.

F As the track bends left, go straight ahead along a fenced track signposted Badbury Rings.

Badbury Rings

G Go through trees into the next field, ignoring paths and the track left and right. Here you can glimpse the east side of the Rings. Go ahead with the hedge on your right.

H Turn right along the grassy path, which runs parallel to the road behind trees, to return to the car park.

3 This is another stretch of Ackling Dyke.

4 Badbury Rings is an excellent example of an Iron Age hillfort. It was built about 800 BC and in use until the Roman invasion in AD 43. Some of the ditches are more than 60ft (18m) deep and may have been nearly twice as deep 2000 years ago. The outermost of its three concentric ramparts is nearly a mile in circumference. Despite achieving the peak of its builder's technology, Badbury Rings was one of the first forts captured by the Second Augustan Legion under Vespasian in either AD 43 or 44.

Entrance to Badbury Rings

This is a very attractive walk leading to one of several hills guarding the valley of the River Stour

The footpath round the base of Hod Hill is considered to be one of the prettiest paths in Dorset and the views from the hillfort are wonderful. Its name is of some significance to ley-hunters and followers of Alfred Watkins' old straight tracks. Hod recalls the box carried on the shoulder with the aid of a rod – the staff of the original surveyors of these ancient earthworks. These unploughed slopes are rich in flora and fauna; the riverside walk is a special treat.

Hod Hill

View of the Blackmore Vale from Hod Hill

Route instructions

A Park beside the White Horse pub or in Stourpaine. Turn left from the pub and left again down South Holme. Go ahead across Manor Road to Havelins, the road opposite, which crosses the River Iwerne.

B Turn right up Hod Drive. Pass beneath Hod Hill on your right and beside the River Stour on your left.

C Bear right with the track through trees to a road. Turn right just before the road to climb up to a gate. Walk uphill with the trees on your right.

1 The western side of Hod Hill, overlooking the Stour valley, is the steepest side, requiring only a low

bank to defend its summit.

D Cross the stile beside a gate ahead to enter, at the corner, the hillfort used by the Romans. Explore the fort as you make for the bottom right-hand corner.

2 When the Romans captured the Iron Age hillfort of Hod Hill in either AD 43 or 44, Vespasian's Second Legion Augusta built its own fort in the northwestern corner and highest part of the British camp. It was garrisoned by 600 legionary infantry and an auxiliary cavalry unit of 250 men and their horses.

3 Hod Hill is one of the largest of the Dorset

Plan your walk

DISTANCE: 3 miles (4.5km)

TIME: 1½ hours

START/END: ST862094 Stourpaine

TERRAIN: Moderate

MAPS:
OS Explorer 118;
OS Landranger 194

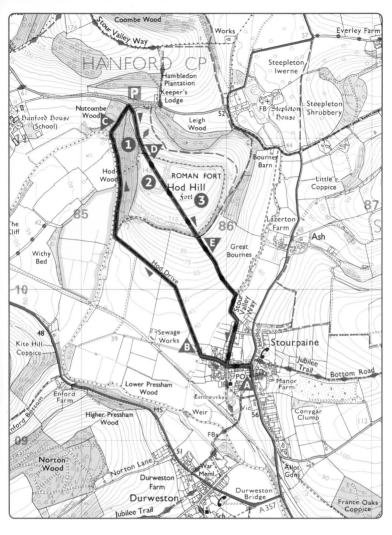

hillforts, with an internal
area of 54 acres (21.9ha)
It was developed over
the whole of the Iron Age,
with ditches and ramparts
being added to make
it impregnable until the
Romans brought their

lethal ballista machine to it
on a movable siege-tower
and rained ballista bolts on
the Durotrigic chieftain's
hut. Slight depressions in
the ground indicate other
British huts set alight by
Roman fire arrows.

Hod Hill

E Cross a stile by a gate and descend along the hedged track back to Stourpaine. Turn right along Manor Road and retrace your steps to your car from the crossroads.

Marsh fritillary

> **❝ This is an easy walk across gentle countryside with pleasant views over Blackmoor Vale ❞**

The route passes along riverside meadows and through delightful wooded areas full of flora and fauna. Sturminster Newton itself is a small market town tucked into a bend of the River Stour. It takes its name from its church (minster) on this river. The locals know it as Stur and it is the gateway to the Vale of Blackmoor, a wide clay vale watered by deep springs in a narrow band of green-sand soil at the foot of the steep chalk downland.

Sturminster Newton

Sturminster Newton Mill

Route instructions

A From the Station Road car park follow the main road through the town centre. Turn left at the museum, just past Market Cross, then turn right along the lane to the church. Follow a path to the left of the church and at a T-junction beyond it, turn left between houses to a lane. Turn right then left along the track signposted Fiddleford Manor & Mill.

B Go through a gate and bear right to follow a path across the fields. Turn left through another gate and continue across the watermeadows. Turn left over a footbridge and bear right to go through a kissing-gate. Cross two more footbridges over

the river and continue to Fiddleford Mill. Turn right by the mill to continue ahead to a lane. Turn left.

1 Fiddleford Mill is a former corn mill. It is no longer working, but it still contains some of its machinery.

2 Fiddleford Manor dates back to the 14th century. It is administered by English Heritage and is open to the public.

C Bear right by a wooden seat to follow a path with a stream on your right. Continue ahead when you reach a tarmac drive. Turn right to follow the lane to the main road. Turn right and just after crossing a

Plan your walk

DISTANCE: 4½ miles (7km)

TIME: 2¼ hours

START/END: ST787142 Sturminster Newton

TERRAIN: Easy

MAPS:
OS Explorer 129;
OS Landranger 194

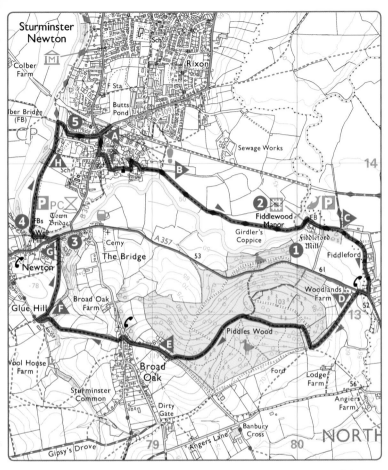

bridge over the stream,
turn left at a footpath sign
to climb a stile beside a
metal gate.

D Walk uphill, keeping
the fence and hedge on
your right. Climb another
stile and continue along
the right-hand edge of the
next field with woodland on
your right. Before reaching
the corner of the field,
turn right through a gate

signposted Broad Oak
to enter Piddles Wood.
Some of this woodland
is managed as a nature
reserve by Dorset Wildlife
Trust. Follow a track
through the wood and at a
fork take the left-hand track.
Follow signs to Broad Oak
until you reach a lane.

E Turn right along the lane
and at a T-junction cross the
road and go down a track to

Sturminster Newton

a kissing-gate. Go through and follow a fenced path across a field, soon joining and keeping by a hedge on the right. Go through a kissing-gate and continue between trees down to cross a footbridge. Head uphill to a lane and immediately turn sharp right onto a narrow, hedge-lined path.

▶ Go through a gate, bear right and, walking with the fence on your right, make for a metal gate at the far side of the field. Go through the gate; keep ahead across rough pasture. Go through another gate along the right-hand edge of the pasture. Go through a kissing-gate and down steps, turn sharp right down to the road opposite Town Bridge.

❸ Town Bridge was built in the late 15th century and was widened in the 17th century. The arched causeway approach was added in the 18th century. It bears a metal plaque threatening deportation to anyone damaging the bridge.

▶ Turn left and then turn right down to the mill. Go round the side of the mill, cross two footbridges and then go ahead through a kissing-gate. Follow a path across the meadows, go through a kissing-gate and continue along the left-hand edge of a recreation ground. Go through another kissing-gate to the left of a large house.

❹ The existence of watermills at Sturminster is recorded in the Domesday Survey of 1086. It is likely that one of these was the predecessor of the present mill. Sturminster Newton Mill is one of the few remaining working water mills in Dorset. The majority of the mill building is late 17th century and was restored to full working order in 1981 by the Mill Trust. It is open to the public during the summer months. Notice the flood-level markings from 1756 and 1979 on the main door.

▶ Continue past the house and descend to the riverside. At a signpost to Market Cross turn right and head uphill by a hedge and fence on your right. Bear right to a kissing-gate. Go through onto a lane and back to the centre of Sturminster Newton.

❺ The small market town of Sturminster Newton was the *Stourcastle* of Thomas Hardy's novels. He lived here from July 1876 to March 1878, describing them as the happiest two years of his married life with Emma. Hardy wrote *The Return of the Native* here, plus several poems.

> **❝** A varied walk starting at Evershot which, at an altitude of 700ft (180m), is the second highest village in Dorset **❞**

The route follows tracks and paths to Melbury Osmond. It can be muddy in parts so it is advisable to wear boots. The walk returns on well-surfaced driveways past Melbury House and through its deer park.

Evershot

Tess' Cottage

Route instructions

A Evershot is at the junction of minor roads 1½ miles (2.4km) west of the A37 where it crosses the Bristol to Weymouth railway line at Holywell. Park at the grassy triangle at the bottom of the hill at the east end of Evershot. Walk into the village, passing Back Lane on your right and following the main road as it bends right into Fore Street, passing Summer Lane on your left.

B Turn right along Back Lane between Tess' Cottage and St Osmond's Church. Follow Back Lane as it bends right to meet the road near your start.

1 St John's Well is on your right about 200yds (180m)

from the church down Back Lane. This is the source of the River Frome, which flows through Dorset to reach the sea at Poole Harbour. There is a display and information board at the site of the well.

C Turn left and then fork left towards Melbury House along the private road.

D Fork right up a track. Continue through trees and past water tanks on your left at the top of the hill. Walk down to the bottom of the hill, passing mixed woodland on your left and a conifer plantation between two fields on your right.

E Bear left along the bridleway to Melbury

Plan your walk

DISTANCE: 5 miles (8km)

TIME: 2½ hours

START/END: ST576047 Evershot

TERRAIN: Easy, but sometimes muddy; one gradual climb

MAPS:
OS Explorer 117;
OS Landranger 194

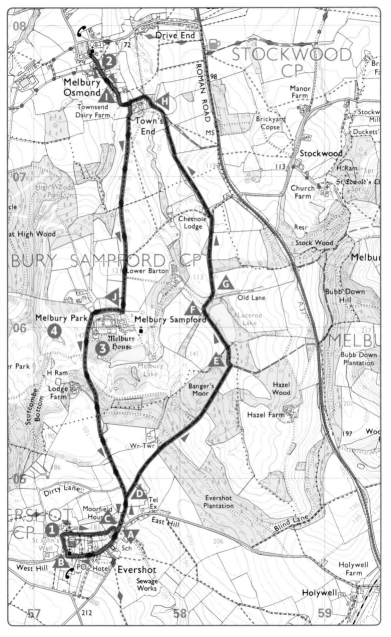

Evershot

Osmond, passing deciduous woodland on your right. Pass through a gate into a field and continue ahead. Look for glimpses of Lucerne Lake through the trees on your right.

F Just after passing a thatched boathouse on your right, go ahead through a gate and turn right, off the main tracks. Bear left through a gate, cross a stream and go through a gate after it.

G Continue ahead with the fence on your right. At the end of the field, turn right through a gate and turn left immediately along a track. Continue through a gate to meet a road as it bends towards a house on your left. Go straight across this road to the track opposite. Continue through a gate at the end of this hedged track and cross a comer of a field to a small gate ahead.

H Continue along the hedged track, which soon bears left to cross over a stream by a footbridge and then bear right. Go under an archway where the path is very muddy, before bearing left to emerge between two thatched cottages at the side of a road.

I Turn right along this road to reach Melbury

Osmond and its church. Retrace your steps and continue to enter the parkland of Melbury House. Go ahead along the private driveway that is also the public path. Keep straight on towards Melbury House.

2 Thomas Hardy's parents' families once owned land around Melbury Osmond. The church was where Hardy's parents, Thomas Hardy (senior) and Jemima Hand, were married on 22nd December 1839. Hardy's mother used to live in the thatched cottage on the north side of the church.

J Just before Melbury House, turn right with the drive and follow it as it bends left and uphill through the deer park. Eventually the drive descends to the road at the grassy triangle where you started.

3 Melbury House is a manor house re-built by Sir Giles Strangways shortly before 1540.

4 Melbury Park is a deer park and has several types of deer – red, fallow and Japanese sika. It is a surviving remnant of the Forest of Blackmoor.

Melbury Osmond Church

> **This walk takes you from Cerne Abbas on to the Downs and past the prehistoric figure of the Cerne Giant on Giant Hill**

Until the 19th century Cerne Abbas was a centre for the leather and brewing industries. Nowadays, it is an appealing village with fine buildings, including some timber-fronted cottages and a 15th century church. It is certainly most famous for its Giant carved into the chalk of the nearby hillside.

Cerne Abbas

Abbey Farm

Route instructions

A Park your car in the 'Cerne Giant Viewpoint' parking area off the A352 north of Cerne Abbas. This is 8 miles (12.8km) north of Dorchester.

Walk with the giant on your left down the lane towards Cerne Abbas.

1 The Cerne Giant is 180ft (55m) high and brandishes a 120ft (36m) club. It has survived the centuries by being regularly scoured and tended by the locals and is now in the care of the National Trust.

The name Cerne may refer to Cernunnos, the Celtic lord of the wild beasts and a giant who wielded a club. The giant was most probably adopted by the Romans when Commodus was emperor (180-93 BC).

The ancient earthwork above the Giant's outstretched arm is the Trendle or Frying Pan. A flat platform may have had a ceremonial purpose. Prisoners may have been kept in the Trendle to await sacrifice in the Beltane fire, perhaps in a wickerwork giant (called a *kolosson* by the Romans).

B Turn left along a lane towards the picnic area. Ignore a path beside the River Cerne on your right but go across the bridge to a T-junction. Turn left to walk for 50yds (45m) then turn right up the hedged path opposite a barn.

Plan your walk

Shepton Mallet · Frome · Trowbridge
· Warminster
Glastonbury
Shaftesbury
Yeovil · Sherborne
· Crewkerne · Blandford Forum
Dorchester
Poole ·
Weymouth · Swanage ·

DISTANCE: 3½ miles (5.5km)

TIME: 1¾ hours

START/END: ST662015 Cerne Giant Viewpoint car park

TERRAIN: Easy / Moderate; one climb up Giant Hill

MAPS: OS Explorer 117; OS Landranger 194

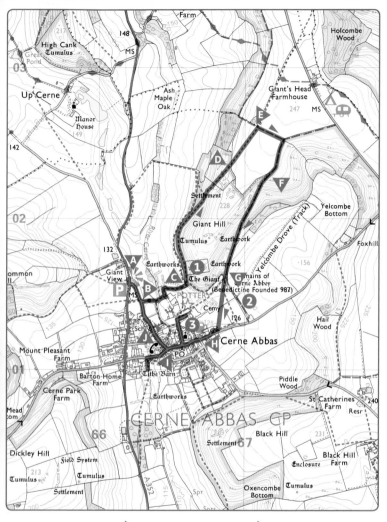

C Go through a gate and bear left up steps to pass under the feet of the giant on your right. Continue parallel with the hedge on your left. Veer right uphill towards trees and scrubland when you reach a cattle trough on your left.

D Cross the stile in the fence ahead. Keep straight on towards the trees on the horizon.

E Turn right along the bridleway across the field. Go ahead through a gate and turn right immediately

Cerne Abbas

to pass through two gates and continue with the hedge on your right.

F Go through another gate and follow the track downhill through scrubland, keeping a fence on your left.

G Near the bottom of the hill ignore the Giants Hill bridleway on your right but then immediately cross a stile on your right. Bear slightly left across the field to a stile just to the right of the sports field. Cross over the stile and continue across the field to reach a gate.

2 The old abbey church stood here. A 9th century monastery was refounded on Benedictine lines in 987 and dissolved by Henry VIII in 1539.

H Go through the gate and follow the path in front of cottages. Turn right along the road (Alton Lane). This leads to Long Street, Cerne Abbas. Ignore Abbey Court on your right but fork right to the parish church of St Mary. Turn right up Abbey Street. Pass the town pond on your right and go on to a gate on your right which leads to the cemetery. Follow the wall on your right and go down to St Augustine's holy well.

3 The parish church of St Mary has an imposing

15th century buttressed tower, a late Norman chancel, heraldic glass and remarkable 14th century wall paintings as well as splendid gargoyles. Around the church there are ruins of the Abbey of Cerne.

I Retrace your steps down Abbey Street to join Long Street. Turn right and continue ahead along The Folly, passing Back Lane on your left. Turn left along the footpath to Boston Meadows to view the 14th century Tithe Barn (now a private residence) on your right.

J Return to the centre of Cerne Abbas and turn left along Duck Street. Follow the road back to the parking area.

Cerne Abbas Pond

> **❝** This is a walk along the great chalk ridge that overlooks Blackmoor Vale. The walk is well off the beaten track. Look out for wild flowers and foxes **❞**

Thomas Hardy described the Dorsetshire Gap in his novel *Tess of the d'Urbervilles* '... the hills are open, the sun blazes down upon the fields so large as to give an unenclosed character to the landscape, the lanes are white, the hedges low and plashed, the atmosphere colourless ... in the valley, the world seems to be constructed upon a smaller and more delicate scale; the fields are mere paddocks ... Arable lands are few and limited; with but slight exceptions the prospect is a broad rich mass of grass and trees, mantling minor trills and dales within the major. Such is the Vale of Blackmoor'.

The Dorsetshire Gap

       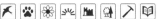

Nettlecombe Tout

Route instructions

Plan your walk

DISTANCE: 2½ miles (4km)

TIME: 1¼ hours

START/END: ST728032 Folly

TERRAIN: Moderate

MAPS:
OS Explorer 117;
OS Landranger 194

A Park at the roadside north of Folly, which is between Piddletrenthide and Mappowder about 10 miles (16km) northeast of Dorchester.

Walk eastwards along a track which crosses the road, passing Folly Farmhouse on your right.

B Ignore a greener track which forks to the right. When your track bears right towards a gate, keep straight on along a narrow bridleway with woodland on your left and a fence on your right.

C When the hedge finishes on your left, go through the gate, turn left and walk towards a prominent water tank. Continue across the field to a small gate in the hedge ahead. Veer slightly right downhill to a gate which leads to a sunken track through woodland. Follow this track which gradually bears right.

D When a similar sunken track comes in to meet yours from the left, turn left along it to a path junction. This is the famous Dorsetshire Gap. To appreciate the view turn right, go through a gate and climb the slope on your left.

1 The Dorsetshire Gap is a quirk of geology, where many steep slopes meet in a small area, as if a giant had folded the chalk like a pocket handkerchief. The

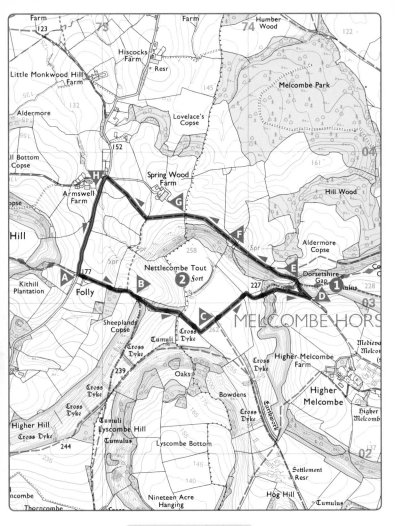

view from the top of the slopes is breathtaking.

E Having enjoyed the view, return to the Dorsetshire Gap junction. Follow the path ahead into the woodland signposted Armswell Farm, with steep banks on your left. Go ahead through a gate, with trees behind a fence on your left, uphill to a gate just after a gap in the hedge.

F Keep straight on with woodland on your left. Go through a double gate,

The Dorsetshire Gap

turn left and cross a track and go through the hunting-gate ahead.

G Bear right across the field to pass through two more waymarked gates. Continue downhill with the hedge on your left. When the hedge bears left, continue ahead across the field to reach the road.

2 Nettlecombe Tout is a fine lookout with a single ancient ditch. The Iron Age Fort seems to have been left uncompleted. Tout was a Celtic god, Romanised to Toutates.

H Turn left along the road back towards Folly and your car.

Sunrise halo in misty Blackmore Vale

> **❝** This easy 5 mile walk explores the valley of the River Piddle and the attractive wooded ridge to the south of it **❞**

Tolpuddle is a place made famous by its Martyrs. They were six agricultural labourers of the village whose trade union meetings led to them being sentenced to seven years' transportation to Australia in 1834 for daring to form a trade union and demand a wage increase. They planned, by withholding their labour, to force farmers to increase their wages from eight shillings to ten shillings a week. If you park near the village green you will see the old sycamore tree under which the Martyrs met.

Tolpuddle

Athelhampton House

Route instructions

 Tolpuddle is on a minor road off the A35 between Puddletown and Bere Regis.

Start from Tolpuddle village green. Walk away from the village green down the lane towards Southover.

B Ignore a waymarked bridleway on your right, bend left with the lane and turn right. Bear left to pass a thatched cottage on your right and continue along a rough, hedged track. Keep to this track, ignoring all turnings. When the track veers to the left continue ahead up another track to enter woodland.

C Turn right at the cross-tracks. Follow this track, ignoring all turnings, until

the track ends at a gate on your left.

D Turn right after the gate and continue with the hedge on your right and a fine view across the Frome valley on your left. Pass a conifer plantation on your right. Go ahead through a gate into an oak wood and immediately turn to follow the narrow path near the fence on your left.

E Turn left through a small gate and turn right to pass a thatched cottage. Continue down the cottage track, turn right towards the farm and then immediately right through a waymarked metal farm gate. Continue up the field to a gate into the wood. Follow the hollow

Plan your walk

DISTANCE: 5 miles (8km)

TIME: 2½ hours; allow extra time to visit Athelhampton House

START/END: SY792945 Tolpuddle village green

TERRAIN: Easy

MAPS: OS Explorer OL 15; OS Landranger 194

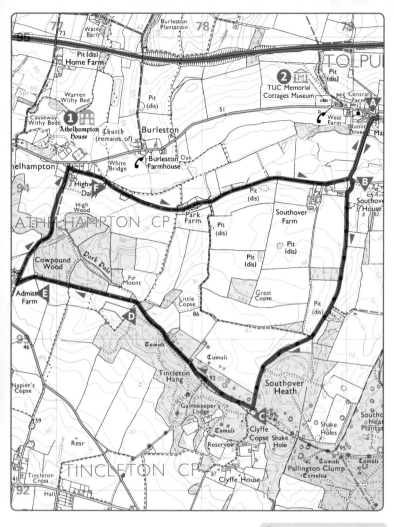

way, ignoring cross-paths down to Athelhampton. Turn left along the road. Athelhampton House is on your right. After visiting the house and gardens, retrace your steps along the main road. Turn left along a path behind the church.

1 Athelhampton is a 15th century mansion with 16th century additions. It was damaged by fire in 1992 but most parts of the building remain on display to the public. Visit the Great Hall, Great Chamber, Wine Cellar and King's Room. The

Tolpuddle

beautiful grounds contain eight walled gardens, fountains, pavilions and topiary pyramids.

▶ At the end of this track go ahead along a path to walk with the hedge on your left. Continue through a waymarked gate through Park Farm to go ahead along a lane. When the lane bends right go ahead through a waymarked gate. Proceed to a small gate in the far left-hand corner of the field and go straight ahead through two gates to access a lane. Turn left to return to Tolpuddle.

2 Tolpuddle Martyrs Museum was built in 1934 by the TUC in memory of the six agricultural workers who were transported to Australia in 1834.

Gardens at Athelhampton House

The area has many associations with the life of author Thomas Hardy who was born here in 1840, grew up and wrote two of his most famous novels – *Under the Greenwood Tree* (1872) and *Far from the Madding Crowd* (1874) in this cottage. The walk also takes in views of Kingston Maurward House and an Elizabethan manor house.

Hardy's Cottage

Hardy's Cottage

Plan your walk

Trowbridge
Shepton Frome
Mallet Warminster
Glastonbury
Shaftesbury
Yeovil Sherborne
• Crewkerne Blandford Forum
Dorchester
Poole
Weymouth Swanage

DISTANCE: 3½ miles (5.5km)

TIME: 1¾ hours

START/END: SY726922 Thorncombe Wood car park, Higher Bockhampton

TERRAIN: Easy

MAPS:
OS Explorer OL 15;
OS Landranger 194

Route instructions

A Start the walk from the car park for Hardy's Cottage, which is in Higher Bockhampton.

Follow the signposted woodland path to Hardy's cottage, bearing left uphill from the car park. Ignore a path on your right but continue to a signpost where you turn left, then bear right. Turn left down to Hardy's cottage.

1 Thomas Hardy was born in this cottage on 2nd June 1840. You can view the interior, including the bedroom where Hardy was born. It is owned by the National Trust and open from the end of April to the end of October, except Tuesdays and Wednesdays.

B Turn left around Hardy's cottage to walk down Bockhampton Lane. Pass the turn for the car park on your left and go ahead to the road (Cuckoo Lane). Turn left along it for 50yds (45m) then turn right up the waymarked, hedged track, referred to as a 'drong' in Hardy's novels. When it bears right, keep straight on through a gate into a field to walk with a fence on your right. The Admiral Hardy monument is straight ahead on the horizon.

2 The view of Admiral Hardy's monument must have interested his namesake. Hardy introduced his remote ancestor into his historical novel *The Trumpet Major*.

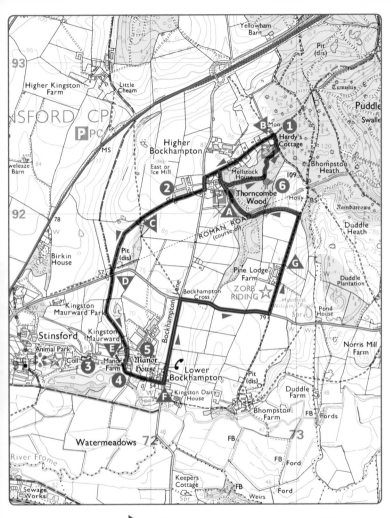

C Go through a waymarked gate and follow the well-trodden path straight ahead across the middle of the field to a track where you turn left to reach a minor road.

D Cross the road and continue along the fenced

waymarked bridleway ahead. As it bears left there is a view of Kingston Maurward House and Park on your right. Go through a gate to cross a track to a gate ahead on your left. Follow a track to a gate which gives access to a lane.

Hardy's Cottage

▶ Turn right and then left at the junction, keeping the Elizabethan manor house on your left. Go through a gate beside a cattle grid. Continue past the walled demonstration garden of Kingston Maurward College on your left. Walk past the bungalows of Knapwater on your left to reach the old schoolhouse on your left.

❸ Kingston Maurward House is an extravagant manor built close to an older one between 1717 and 1720 by George Pitt, who married Lora Grey, the last heiress of a longstanding local family. It is encased in dressed Portland stone because George II regretted it was 'built of b-b-brick'. The owner went bankrupt to please the King. Julia Augusta Martin lived here. She founded the village school (Hardy was its first pupil) and took a maternal interest in the young Hardy.

❹ The old manor house dates from the late 16th century.

❺ The old schoolhouse in Lower Bockhampton is where Hardy spent his first year at school at the age of seven. He then went to school in Dorchester.

▶ Turn left to follow the road through Lower Bockhampton. Go ahead to a crossroads, where you turn right towards Tincleton. Turn left after ½ mile (0.8km) along the track to Pine Lodge Farm.

◀ Pass Pine Lodge Farm and Tea Rooms on your left and go ahead through two gates. Cross a stile and follow a narrow path between a hedge on your left and a fence on your right to the wood ahead. Cross another stile and turn left along the path. Descend to a gate and bear left down a track to reach the car park.

❻ Thornecombe Wood and Black Heath together form a 66 acre (26.4ha) nature reserve. Look for a ridge crossing your path in Thornecombe Wood. This is the course of Ackling Dyke, the Roman road from Durnovaria (Dorchester) to Londinium (London) via Badbury Rings and Old Sarum. The ghost of a Roman centurion has been seen here, his feet elevated to the road's former height.

" A dramatic walk along Golden Cap, the highest cliff on the south coast of England **"**

The scenery is magnificent and the views are extensive, from Chesil Beach and the Isle of Portland in the east, to Lyme Regis and Devon in the west.

Golden Cap

View from Golden Cap

Route instructions

① Seatown is situated in a gap in the cliffs overlooking a shingle beach. It has an 18th century inn.

A Start from the car park (charge) near the beach of Seatown. This is at the end of Sea Hill Lane, which runs south from the A35 opposite the church in Chideock. Turn right out of the car park and walk up Sea Hill Lane to cross a stile on the left.

B Walk along a narrow path to a gate. Bear left across the field to another gate and cross a footbridge. Follow the gravel path through woodland. Cross a stile and go through a gate ahead. Walk uphill to a signpost by a bench.

C Turn right and follow the well-trodden path uphill and then bear left through scrubland. Cross a stile and continue along the South West Coast Path across an open field to a signpost beside a bench. Cross the stile and continue ahead to reach a gate in the fence on your left. Go through to climb the stepped path to the summit of Golden Cap.

② At 618ft (188m), Golden Cap is the highest cliff along the south coast. It is named after its flat summit of golden sandstone. The National Trust has achieved the conservation of 6 miles (9.6km) of rugged cliffs in its Golden Cap Estate. Lord Antrim, the chairman of the National Trust from 1966

Plan your walk

Shepton Mallet · Frome · Trowbridge
Warminster
Glastonbury
Shaftesbury
Yeovil · Sherborne
· Crewkerne
Blandford Forum
Dorchester
Poole
Weymouth
Swanage

DISTANCE: 3 miles (5km)

TIME: 2 hours

START/END: SY419917 Seatown car park

TERRAIN: Strenuous; three steep climbs

MAPS:
OS Explorer 116;
OS Landranger 193

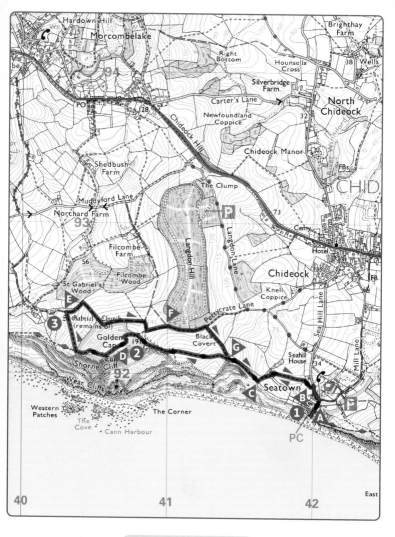

until his death in 1977, is remembered by a memorial at the summit.

D Follow the South West Path from the Ordnance Survey triangulation pillar to the memorial stone to Lord Antrim. Continue downhill to a signpost, where you bear right downhill to a ruined church (St Gabriel's).

3 The ruined church at Stanton St Gabriel testifies to the former existence of

Golden Cap

a thriving community here. There were twenty-three families living in cottages around the village green in 1650, but the population gradually shifted to nearby Morcombelake. Finally, in 1824, the road was re-routed through Morcombelake.

▶ Retrace your steps and fork left steeply uphill to follow the signposted bridleway. Keep the hedge on your left until you go through a gate. Turn right and walk uphill right around the edge of this field to a gate in its far top corner. Follow the signposted bridleway to Langdon Hill and Seatown.

▶ Go ahead through a gate and bear right along the edge of the wood on Langdon Hill. Turn right over a stile to follow the path to Seatown, which follows a fence on your left to rejoin the Coast Path at a signpost.

▶ Turn left over the stile and retrace your steps to Seatown.

Ruins of St Gabriel Church

66 A hilly walk through farmland, moorland and woods with views to the south coast 99

The monument on this walk is to Sir Thomas Masterman Hardy, who was born at Portesham in 1769. Hardy worked his way up through the Navy ranks and reached the rank of First Sea Lord at the Admiralty in 1830. In 1805, he was Nelson's flag captain at Trafalgar and was to whom Nelson, as he lay dying, made his famous remark 'Kiss me, Hardy'.

The Hardy Monument

Hardy Coppice

Plan your walk

Route instructions

1 The Hardy Monument was erected between 1844 and 1846 (Admiral Hardy died in 1839) and is an ugly octagonal tower over 70ft (21m) high. This is the highest point of Black Down and the view from here is magnificent. On your extreme right is Start Point on the south Devon coast, while the Needles can be seen on your extreme left.

A Park your car below the Hardy Monument, which is by the road between Martinstown and Portesham. With your back to the monument and the sea in front of you walk ahead to the left of the small quarry. Bear left along a distinct path through the heather down to conifers.

B Cross a level forestry track to follow a narrow path through the trees to join the track you previously crossed.

C Turn left and follow the track to a fork.

D From the fork bear left downhill. Go ahead at a cross-track at the edge of the forest to descend to a signpost for Portesham, just before the ruin of Black Down Barn.

E Turn left and go through a gate uphill with a fence on your left. Pass a gate and trees on your right and go ahead through a gate. Continue with a fence on your left and a wall on your right.

DISTANCE: 3½ miles (5.5km)

TIME: 1¾ hours

START/END: SY613876 Hardy Monument

TERRAIN: Moderate

MAPS:
OS Explorer OL 15;
OS Landranger 194

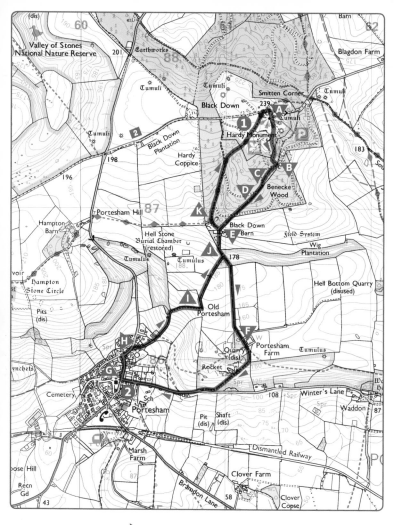

F Pass a farm on your left, go through a gate ahead to follow a track which bends right downhill to a road. Turn right to reach Portesham.

2 Read the interesting epitaph on the outside of

St Peter's Church, Portesham, which refers to the Civil War.

G Your way is on the right, up the road signposted to Hardy's Monument. First, however, visit Portesham church on your left. Bear

The Hardy Monument

right past Portesham Stores.

▶ Fork right along the bridleway signposted 'Hardy Monument 1¼'. Go along a hedged track to a gate then keep to the left side of a field as you climb uphill. Follow the distinct track as it swings right.

▶ Turn left along the walled track at the top of the field. Go through the gate. Bear right and continue ahead with the wall on your right to pass through two more gates.

▶ Turn left along the track you followed on your outward journey. This time, however, fork left just past the barn to a second signpost.

▶ Bear right along the uphill path through the trees, ignoring tracks on your right until a right fork is signposted 'Hardy Monument ¼'. Go ahead to the monument and car park.

St Peter's Church

> **❝** This easy walk is through a page of the unwritten history of Wessex. It takes you to Maiden Castle, one of the greatest Iron Age hillforts in Britain **❞**

The impressive earthworks of the Castle are easily accessible. It has triple banks and ditches enclosing 45 acres (18ha). It was at its peak in the final century before the Roman invasion, when it was the chief settlement of the Durotriges, the tribe which held Dorset. They were prosperous, with wheat production then rivalling yields attained in the Second World War. About 5,000 of them lived in this hillfort. Excavators have found traces of their huts and numerous grain storage pits. Their defences were the peak of Iron Age technology, perhaps earning the hillfort its 'maiden' label for impregnability. Their chief weapon was the sling, and an ammunition stockpile totalling 54,000 pebbles from Chesil Beach has been found.

Maiden Castle

Roman Temple remains

Route instructions

A Start from the car park at Maiden Castle, which is signposted from the A354 on the southern outskirts of Dorchester. Walk up the track through two gates to enter the hillfort by the western entrance through a maze of banks and ditches.

B Go ahead from the gateway across the interior, bearing slightly left to reach a hollow which once contained a dew pond. After the Roman period, the hilltop was used to graze stock and dew ponds were created to provide water.

1 Maiden Castle is certainly the best-known hillfort in England. Here you cross the ditch and bank of an earlier, simpler earthwork

that enclosed just 10 acres (4ha) at the eastern end of Maiden Castle.

C Cross the bank barrow ahead and veer slightly left to see the remains of a Romano-British temple. Climb the top rampart, with its excellent view over Dorchester and the new town of Poundbury. Continue along the rampart to the eastern entrance.

2 This Romano-British temple dates from about AD 370, nearly 200 years after the fort was abandoned.

D Inspect the double gateways at the eastern entrance to the hillfort. Continue along the southern ramparts.

Plan your walk

DISTANCE: 2 miles (3km)

TIME: 1 hour

START/END: SY669889 Maiden Castle car park

TERRAIN: Easy; with a gradual climb to the hillfort

MAPS: OS Explorer OL 15; OS Landranger 194

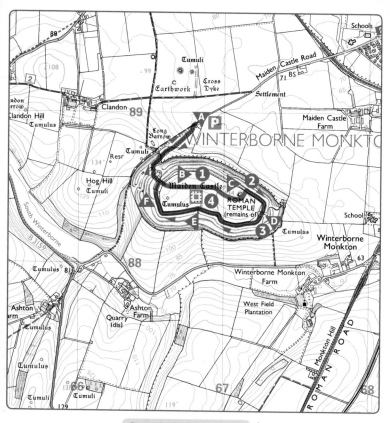

3 Excavations by Sir Mortimer Wheeler in the 1930s revealed the complete eastern entrance had been enlarged and modified over time. He also found a late Iron Age cemetery of more than fifty-two burials.

E Pass a circular hollow on your right thought to mark a well.

4 The separate ramparts have a relationship of distance and height to each other that was carefully calculated and engineered.

F On reaching the western gateway retrace your steps to your car.

Finds from the site can be seen in the excellent Dorset County Museum in High West Street, Dorchester. The museum is run by the Dorset Natural History and Archaeological Society and is a delight for geologists, archaeologists and lovers of natural history.

Maiden Castle

Maiden Castle

> **❝** This walk affords lovely views over Weymouth and the South Coast **❞**

The 4½ miles (7.2km) walk takes you up on to White Horse Hill to see the chalk carving of King George III on his white horse.

White Horse Hill

Sutton Poyntz

Shepton Mallet · Frome · Trowbridge

· Warminster

Glastonbury

Shaftesbury

Yeovil · Sherborne

· Crewkerne · Blandford Forum

Dorchester

Poole

Weymouth · Swanage

DISTANCE: 4½ miles (7km)

TIME: 2¼ hours

START/END: SY707838 Sutton Poyntz

TERRAIN: Moderate; one long steep climb

MAPS:
OS Explorer OL 15;
OS Landranger 194

Route instructions

A From Weymouth turn left off the A353 at Preston for Sutton Poyntz, then fork right to the Springhead Inn. Park near the mill pond.

Cross the bridge upstream of the pond and turn left to pass the pond on your left. Continue along the park beside the stream to the mill, passing a footbridge and a seat on your left.

B Turn left around the mill and walk past the pond again towards the downs ahead. Turn right along the signposted track and turn left at another footpath sign.

C Go through a gate and continue ahead across the field to a kissing-gate in its far right-hand corner. Bear

slightly right uphill to join a track. Follow the track, which bears slightly left to the top of the down.

D Turn right through a gate and follow the bridleway to Osmington. Divert right from the path immediately after the next gate to see the Osmington White Horse carved on the hillside. Return to your path to walk with a hedge on your left along the top of the field to a gate ahead.

1 The Osmington White Horse covers more than an acre and is the only chalk horse figure with a rider. It was made in 1808, and is of King George III who regularly visited Weymouth. Apparently the King did

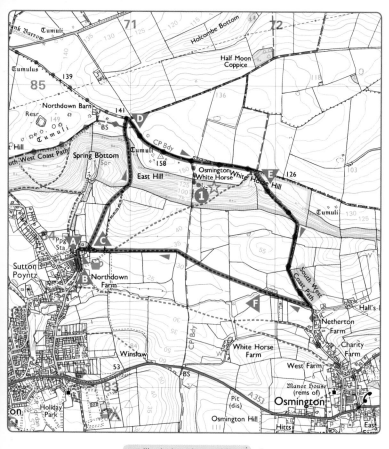

not like being shown riding away from Weymouth and never visited again.

E ▶ Bear right along the track downhill towards the village of Osmington, crossing a stile by a gate on the way. Shortly after the track crosses a stream, go through a gate on the right waymarked Sutton Poyntz. The hedge is on your left and the stream on your right, with the White Horse in view on the hillside.

Bear right through a gap in the hedge, next to an old footbridge, where the stream runs through a pipe.

F ▶ Bear slightly right across the field to a gate in a hedge. Continue to a gate and a stile and then across the corner of the field to another stile. Keep the hedge on your left as you continue ahead. Pass through two gates to reach the lane leading back to the start.

White Horse Hill

Countryside looking towards Maiden Castle

View towards Weymouth Bay

66 A pleasant walk with sea views, starting in the picturesque village of Abbotsbury 99

Abbotsbury is set in rolling countryside between the downs and Chesil Beach. Its unspoilt thatched cottages made it the ideal location for scenes in the film of Thomas Hardy's *Far from the Madding Crowd*. The famous Swannery is open from April to October seven days a week.

Abbotsbury Swannery

Swans at Abbotsbury Swannery

Route instructions

A Park your car in the car park signposted on your left as you enter Abbotsbury on the B3157 from Weymouth. Leave the car park by the walled track towards the church.

B Turn left through a kissing-gate into the churchyard. Turn right to pass the church on your left. Turn left around the church and fork right to a small gate. Continue through a gap in the fence to see the remains of Abbotsbury Abbey. Go ahead to the old mill pond and turn right to a lane.

1 Notice two medieval stone coffins in the churchyard opposite the porch of St Nicholas' Church.

The porch contains the carved effigy of an abbot dating from about 1200.

2 South of the churchyard gate is the Pynion End, the best part of the abbey remains. This wall dates from about 1400 and incorporates a fireplace.

C Turn right up this lane (Church Street) to the village. Bear left up Market Street.

D Turn left up Chapel Lane, a rough waymarked track, towards the chapel on the hill ahead. Where Chapel Lane bends right, go ahead through a kissing-gate and bear right past farm buildings on your right. Continue uphill to reach the chapel.

Plan your walk

DISTANCE: 2½ miles (4km)

TIME: 1¼ hours

START/END: SY579852 Abbotsbury

TERRAIN: Easy / Moderate; one climb up to the Chapel

MAPS: OS Explorer OL 15; OS Landranger 194

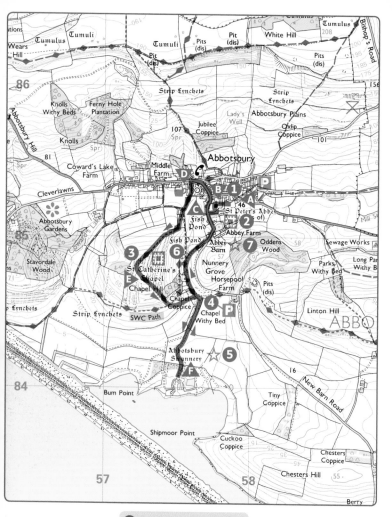

3 St Catherine's Chapel was retained as a landmark for sailors after the dissolution of the monasteries. It is built entirely of stone, roof and all, with heavy buttresses and thick walls.

E On the far side of the chapel go through a gate and bear left to the right hand edge of a coppice. Walk downhill with the coppice on your left to cross a stile in a stone wall. Go on across a stile in the next hedge and then over the stream. Turn right to the Swannery for which there is an admission charge.

Abbotsbury Swannery

4 The withy bed is where willow is grown to be pollarded annually when the 6ft (1.8m) stems are used to tie up reed bundles.

5 The Swannery was established by the monks in the 14th century. About 600 mute swans breed here.

F Walk back past the withy bed to the Swannery car park. Follow the track on your left, signposted 'Coastal Path', past the old mill. Continue to the mill pond and retrace your steps to the car park.

6 The building with a millstone against its wall was the abbey mill.

7 The tithe barn is the largest in Britain. Built by the abbey monks in the 14th century, it is now used by Abbotsbury Children's Farm.

Abbotsbury

“ A walk of special interest to children, since it explores the setting of a children's classic: *Moonfleet*, by the author John Meade Falkner **”**

The route takes you along a coastal path beside Chesil Beach and the Fleet Lagoon to Moonfleet, where you can descend to the beach at Gore Cove. Chesil Beach and the Fleet Lagoon are important areas for their wildlife. The Fleet Lagoon is the second oldest nature reserve in the country and has been protected for its mute swans, which are in abundance at the Abbotsbury Swannery (Walk 15). Many sea birds breed on the beach.

Moonfleet

Chesil Beach and
Fleet Lagoon at sunset

Route instructions

A Park at Holy Trinity
Church, Fleet. This church
is on your right as you drive
along the lane to Fleet from
the B3157 at Chickerell,
northwest of Weymouth,
well-served by town buses.
If you travel by bus, walk
down the lane from
Chickerell towards Fleet,
but start the walk at **B**.
If you drive to the church,
walk back down the lane to
the corner where it turns left.

1 Just a few cottages
remain of the original hamlet
of East Fleet, since it was
virtually destroyed by a
terrible storm on 23rd
November 1824. The
chancel of the old church
was spared. Beneath it is
the Mohun family vault and
an old smugglers' secret

passage. A brass
plaque on the south wall
commemorates John Meade
Falkner. Robert Mohun
acquired Fleet in 1566. His
son, Maximilian, probably
rebuilt the church to
incorporate the family vault.
The Mohuns were royalists
who had their estate
confiscated in the Civil War,
although it was returned to
them at the Restoration.
They remained loyal to the
Stuarts even when William
of Orange landed. Robert
Mohun (born 1715) was the
last male heir, and Fleet
passed, by marriage, to the
Gould family. The heir to
their fortune in 1818 was the
bachelor Reverend George
Gould, who was Rector of
Fleet when the great storm
destroyed his church.

Plan your walk

DISTANCE: 4 miles
(6.5km)

TIME: 2 hours

START/END: SY632805
Fleet

TERRAIN: Easy

MAPS:
OS Explorer OL 15;
OS Landranger 194

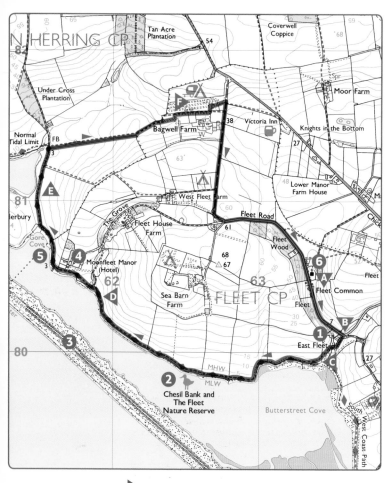

B From the corner follow the path to Old Fleet Church, passing cottages on your right. Go through a gate on your right to visit the old church. Return to the path and turn right through a gate. Bear right around the churchyard wall and then bear left.

C Ignore a gate on your left but go through a gate on your right to walk with the Fleet lagoon and Chesil Beach on your left. Continue through a gate and over a footbridge along a narrow hedged path to a second field. When you reach a wall continue ahead through a gate. Walk along this coastal path until you reach a thicket where there is a Coast Path signpost to Abbotsbury.

Moonfleet

2 The Fleet is a lagoon between the mainland and Chesil Beach. It is a shallow stretch of water containing a lot of weed. Eels, bass and mullet abound, but may only be fished by a few locals. The Fleet has been a protected reserve since the 14th century. The east end of the Fleet is salty and tidal, but it becomes brackish and still in the west.

3 The Dorset coastline here is dominated by Chesil Beach, a barrier of pebbles connecting the Isle of Portland with the mainland. It is over 17 miles (27km) long and the stones increase in size towards the east. The stones come from as far away as Cornwall and have been mixed up by the tides. The Isle of Portland acts as a huge groyne to prevent the pebbles moving on. Chesil Beach acts as a reef protecting the coastline behind it from erosion.

D Turn left through the gate down a hedged duckboarded path and across a footbridge. Continue across the field ahead to pass the Moonfleet Hotel. Continue past the noticeboard about the Fleet Nature Reserve. Pass through a gate and another thicket to reach Gore Cove.

4 Part of the Moonfleet Hotel was the Mohun family manor house.

5 *Moonfleet* by John Meade Falkner is a tale of smuggling on this coast involving the local Mohun family. Thomas Hardy's grandfather was involved in the smuggling business, which was a common activity in these parts.

E Go through a gate in a wall and veer right to walk with the wall on your right. Ignore a signpost to West Fleet Campsite but continue to the next Coast Path signpost. Leave the Coast Path here by turning right through a gap in the wall, then immediately right for a few paces to turn left to follow the footpath to Bagwell Farm Campsite, with the hedge on your left.

F Enter the campsite and keep the hedge on your left until the path turns left to leave the hedge on your right and the site shop on your left. Walk past a playground on your right to a stile in the campsite fence ahead. Turn right along a track, which bears left to a lane. Turn left down this lane back to Fleet.

6 Fleet's new church was completed in 1829 at the vicar's expense. The apsidal chancel has a vaulted plaster roof and contains a large marble monument with mourning figures. It contains the old church bell.

Holy Trinity Church

❝ This easy route is not a circular walk, but a frequent bus service from Weymouth to Portland stops at either end of the route **❞**

The Isle of Portland is not really an island, since it is connected to the mainland by Chesil Beach. As the southernmost point of Dorset it gives fine views of the English Channel. Portland is part of the Jurassic Coast, which is a World Heritage site on the Dorset coast, important for its geology and landforms.

Portland

Coastline of the Isle of Portland

Route instructions

A Park at the Museum and Church Ope car park on the right just past Portland Museum. From the museum, go down Church Ope Road which becomes a footpath and which passes Rufus Castle on your right. Go down steps towards the beach. When the steps turn left, turn right along a narrow, hedged path signposted to a 13th century church.

1 Portland Museum houses the Island's Shipwreck and Smuggling story. It is housed in Avice's Cottage, a 17th century building featured in Thomas Hardy's novel *The Well Beloved*.

B Go up steps past the ruins of St Andrew's Church. Turn right under an old arch

and continue through trees. Pass Pennsylvania Castle on your left. Turn left along the road.

2 Church Ope Cove is the only natural landing-place on the island.

C Turn right along Weston Street for 250yds (225m). Turn right along a signposted footpath.

D Turn left along the track to an old windmill. Fork right to a second old windmill. Bear right, then turn left beside the line of a dismantled railway. Pass a school on your left. Cross a road to continue along a path ahead, which reaches the corner of a road at a footpath signpost.

DISTANCE: 2½ miles (4km)

TIME: 1¼ hours

START/END: SY695712 Museum and Church Cope car park

TERRAIN: Easy

MAPS:
OS Explorer OL 15;
OS Landranger 194

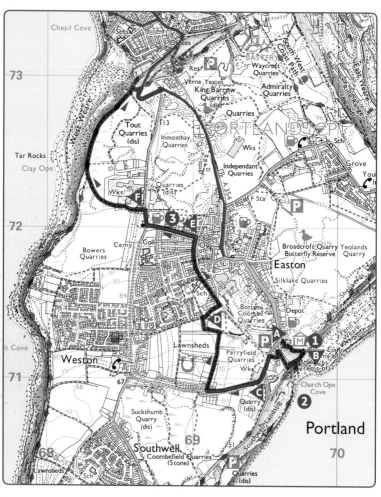

E Turn left along the third road on your left (the main road through the village of Reforne). Pass the George Inn on your left to reach St George's Church at the head of the road. Turn right along Wide Street for 150yds (135m).

3 The George Inn was

where the 'Court Leet' (local council) met.

F Turn left along a signposted footpath. Bear right towards the cliffs. When you reach the road near a sharp bend, turn right up the road to reach a bus stop just beyond the roundabout.

Portland

Church Ope Cove

> **This lovely walk affords beautiful views of the Dorset coast**

The walk follows a section of the South West Coast Path which includes Durdle Door, one of the highlights of this coastal walk. The views are tremendous, from Portland Bill in the west, to St Aldhelm's Head in the east. The return route is along downland paths.

Durdle Door

Lulworth Cove

Route instructions

1 Lulworth Cove can be seen as you rest or look back on your initial climb up the path to the clifftop from the car park. It features in Thomas Hardy's writings as 'Lulwind Cove' and is where the dashing but ruthless Sergeant Troy is thought to have drowned in *Far from the Madding Crowd*.

A Lulworth Cove is at the end of the B3070, 5 miles (8km) south of Wool. Walk from the car park, with Lulworth Cove behind you, along a clear, chalky, track.

B Go through a gate. Bear left along the track to the top of the cliff. This is the South West Coast Path, which you follow for 1 mile (1.6km) until you see the

natural arch of Durdle Door jutting out towards Portland across Weymouth Bay.

2 The natural rock archway of Durdle Door was formed by the sea wearing away the softer clays that join the promontory to the main cliff.

C Retrace your steps past Durdle Door, now on your right, to a low waymark stone.

D Fork left uphill along the path to the caravan site. A fence joins your path from the right. Ignore a stile in it, and the one after, to go through a gate ahead.

E Turn right through a gate waymarked West Lulworth Youth Hostel. Bear left to

Plan your walk

DISTANCE: 2¾ miles (4.5km)

TIME: 2 hours

START/END: SY820801 Lulworth Cove and Heritage Centre car park

TERRAIN: Moderate; one steep climb

MAPS: OS Explorer OL 15; OS Landranger 194

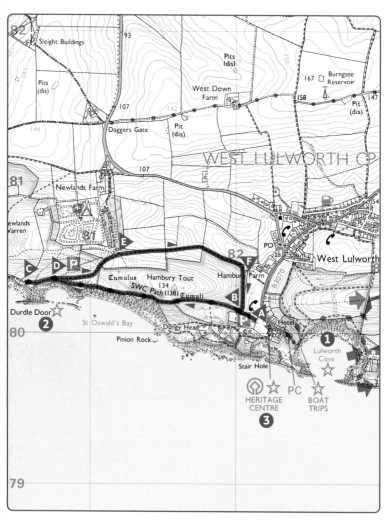

walk beside the hedge on your left. Continue with the fence on your left, passing through a gate on the way.

F Ignore a gate on your left. Continue to Lulworth Cove car park. Then visit the Lulworth Heritage Centre.

3 Lulworth Heritage Centre has permanent exhibitions and displays of local geology and history.

Durdle Door

St Oswald's Bay

> 66 The ruins of Corfe Castle are a splendid sight. Standing high on a hill, the Castle guards the only gap in the Purbeck Hills, with mellowed stone cottages grouped in the village below 99

This walk takes you to Knowle Hill and then back along the ridge path to Corfe Castle itself. The ruins of Corfe Castle are fundamentally Norman, but this was the site of a Saxon lodge where the scheming Elfrida had her stepson Edward the Martyr murdered in 978. The Saxons were punished for this crime with the rule of Elfrida's natural son, Ethelred the Unready. King John extended the castle in the early 13th century. Queen Elizabeth I gave it to Sir Christopher Hatton, a Lord Chancellor in the 16th century. Sir John Bankes, Attorney-General to King Charles I, purchased the castle eight years before the Civil War. The resolute Lady Bankes twice withstood sieges before her tiny garrison was forced to surrender in 1646.

Knowle Hill, near Corfe Castle

Corfe Castle

Corfe Castle

Route instructions

A Park in the car park (pay and display) signposted off West Street, Corfe Castle.

Look for a gate on your right from the car park and follow the path down to a footbridge over the River Corfe.

B Cross the bridge and bear left to a gate in the fence on your right. Go ahead to the left side of the earthworks which are the remains of a Norman Castle. Go through a gate to give access to the lane. Turn left and proceed for 30yds (27m), then turn right through a gate signposted Knowle Hill. Go ahead uphill to a stile in the fence ahead.

C Turn left along the bridleway. Keep to this

bottom track, with the hedge on your left. Go through two gates ignoring the right fork to Knowle Hill between the two. Pass the lime kiln on your right. Cross a stile and continue until a stile beside a gate on your left invites you to Church Knowle. Instead of going left, however, bear right uphill. Cross a stile and continue to the ridge.

1 Church Knowle lime kiln was restored by the Ramblers' in 1988.

D At the commemorative stone, turn right along the ridge path. Go through a gate and walk with a fence on your left to a gate ahead. Continue towards two round barrows ahead.

Plan your walk

DISTANCE: 3½ miles (5.5km)

TIME: 2 hours

START/END: SY958818 Car park off West Street, Corfe Castle

TERRAIN: Moderate; one steep climb up Knowle Hill

MAPS:
OS Explorer OL 15;
OS Landranger 195

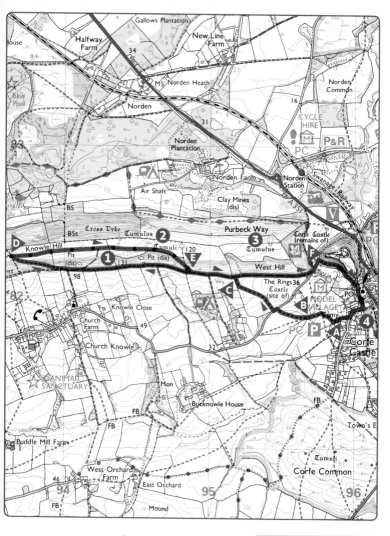

E Follow the path beside the fence on your right to a gate. Bear right downhill to the bottom bridleway. Turn left along it, with a fence and a hedge on your right, all the way to a gate leading to a lane. Turn left over a bridge.

2 A famous ley line runs through tumuli on Knowle Hill and the northern side of Corfe Castle. It strikes the southern side of the northernmost of the two tumuli.

Corfe Castle

3 Here is another tumulus on the Corfe Castle ley line.

Model Village entrance and continue to the car park.

Turn right along a footpath with Corfe Castle above on your left. Emerge near the castle entrance. Turn right past the Cross for West Street. Pass the

4 The village to the south of Corfe Castle was the centre of Purbeck's stone and marble industry in the Middle Ages.

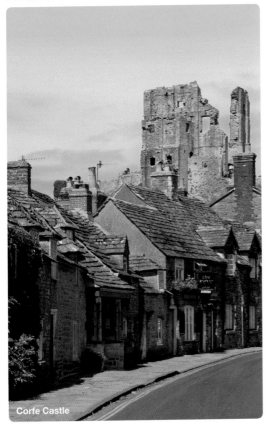

Corfe Castle

> **An easy 4 miles (6.4km) walk, clearly waymarked, along the beautiful Dorset coast**

The walk takes you along the South West Coast Path from Studland Bay, past fascinating geological rock formations. The most prominent of these is the natural arch of Old Harry. The Pinnacles are also impressive. The route then climbs up to the top of the ridge of Ballard Down and then goes inland across fields to return to Studland.

Old Harry

Old Harry

Plan your walk

DISTANCE: 4 miles (6.5km)

TIME: 2 hours

START/END: SZ037825 South Beach Car Park, Studland

TERRAIN: Easy; one gradual climb up Ballard Down

MAPS:
OS Explorer OL 15;
OS Landranger 195

Route instructions

A Studland is at the end the B3351, east of Corfe Castle. A minor road connects it with Swanage and Sandbanks Ferry.

Start at South Beach Car Park (NT), near Bankes Arms Inn. Turn right from this car park along the road past the inn until the road bends right.

B Turn left to follow the waymarked South West Coast Path to Old Harry. Follow this path, with the sea on your left, for 2 miles (3.2km).

1 Old Harry is the bigger and closer of the two rocks at the end of Handfast Point. It is also distinguished by its natural arch. The stump

further out to sea is Old Harry's Wife. These are fine examples of coastal erosion. On a clear day you can see The Needles and the Isle of Wight from here.

2 The two further chalk stumps off the shore south of Old Harry are known as the Pinnacles. A sea cave beneath the water between them is called Parson's Barn on account of its huge size. These are textbook examples of coastal erosion.

C Bear right along the uphill track to the top of the ridge of Ballard Down, with its view of Poole Harbour on your right and Swanage on your left. Go through a

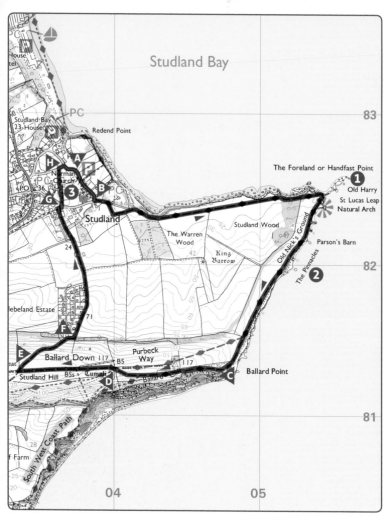

gate on your right to pass a trig point on your right and follow the ridge.

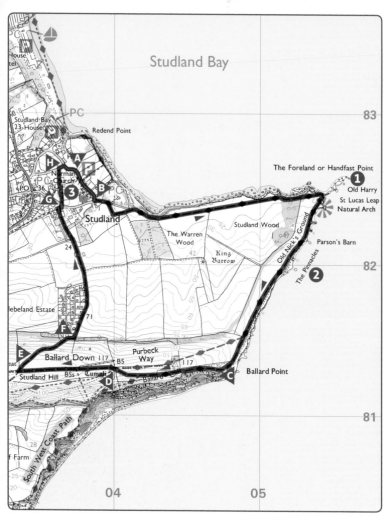 Continue through a gate in the direction of the obelisk.

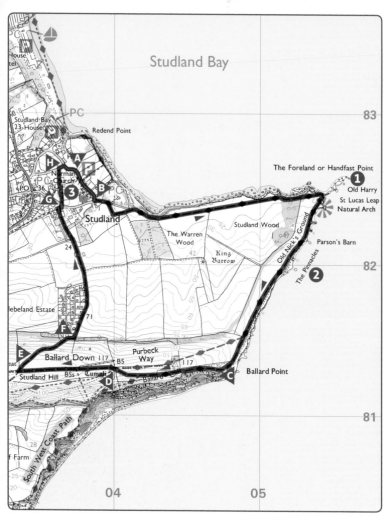 Turn right off the ridge track at the old stone seat

enscribed 'Rest and be thankful'. Continue down to Studland.

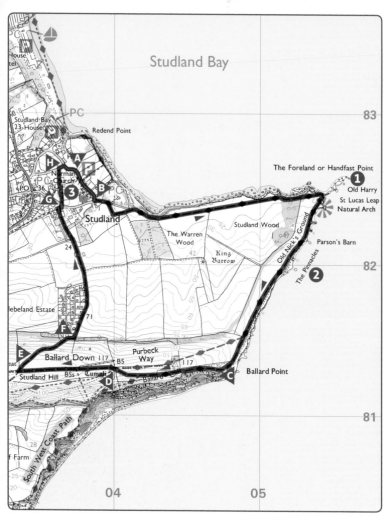 Go through a gate to continue along a lane, ignoring left turnings.

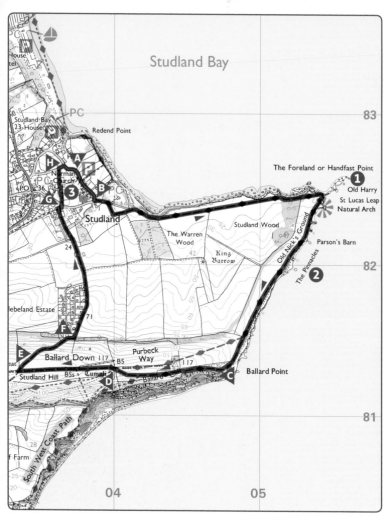 Cross a road to walk up

Old Harry

to the church. Go ahead through the churchyard.

3 The Church of St Nicholas in Studland is almost entirely Norman. Grotesquely carved faces run along the north and south walls of the nave.

Its chalice-shaped font dates from the 12th century, but the carved cross outside is more recent, even showing the aircraft Concorde.

H Turn right along the road back to the car park.

St Nicholas Church

Photo credits

All photographs © HarperCollins Publishers Ltd,
photographer Rosemary MacLeod, with the exception of: